My Ancestry

A Narrative of My Familial Ancestral Past Through Genetic DNA Examination

6/13/2012

Diambu Smith

The cracking of the human genome code is one of the most significant scientific discoveries of the twenty-first century. The ability today is to analyze different aspects of a person's DNA is accredited to this major discovery. DNA tests and sampling are used for a variety of purposes, including the determination of a person's paternity, forensic research for crime scene investigation for police detectives, the analysis of a person's family health history, and now determining a person's ancestral lineage and ethnic admixture. Preparation for the cracking of the human genome code started in the nineteen-nineties with geneticists collecting thousands of human DNA samples from around the world. Howard University became primarily concerned with collecting the DNA samples of many people from various tribes in Africa. The goal was to have millions of people from around the world to find out just what their genetic lineage ancestry was as well as to determine one's genetic ethnic admixture once the human genome was cracked. Now that the human genome code has been cracked, organizations such as African Ancestry and AncestrybyDNA can determine a person's genetic ancestral lineage and estimate a person's genetic ethnic admixture, respectively. As a result of the cracking of the human genome code, and thanks to the aid of the organizations African Ancestry and AncestrybyDNA, I went on my personal research journey to find both my determined genetic ancestral lineage and my estimated genetic ethnic admixture.

One morning, in the spring of 2006, I was listening to the "Tom Joyner Morning Show" on the radio station WZAK 93.1 FM in Cleveland, Ohio, my hometown. It was announced on the show that there existed an organization called African Ancestry that had collected dozens of human DNA samples from the various tribes in Africa. African Ancestry would give people a DNA test by using swabs to collect DNA samples of people from the inside of a person's cheek, and use that sample to test for a match of African tribal DNA samples to determine if a person had genetically African ancestral lineage. African Ancestry was being touted as the organization with the most comprehensive collection of African tribal DNA samples in the world. The organization was deemed as being a primary place for Black Americans to find their African ancestral roots. Finally, a significant connection could be made to the Motherland of Africa for African-Americans once severed from that specific connection by the horrors

4

of slavery in America. The ancestors of millions of Black Americans went from being kidnapped and stolen from Africa to the Middle Passage to being auctioned off as slaves shortly after arriving on American soil. Today, Black Americans can find out for themselves not only if they are of African descent, but also the specific tribe they are related to in Africa and the African nation in which that tribe currently resides thanks to African Ancestry. After listening to that radio broadcast, I determined that I would contact African Ancestry to help me find my genetic ancestral roots.

In the summer of 2006, I purchased both a Matriclan and a Patriclan test kit from African Ancestry for about $620.00. Men, as a result of having both the X chromosome from their mothers and the Y chromosome from their fathers, can find out both their maternal and paternal ancestral lineage. Women, at this point, are only able to find out their maternal ancestral lineage through the X chromosome received from their mothers. Hopefully one day geneticists will be able to find a way to find a woman's paternal ancestral lineage by examining and analyzing the X chromosome given to her by her father. I tested myself in the hopes of finding both my maternal and paternal genetic ancestral lineage.

The results of my Matriclan and Patriclan DNA lineage tests from African Ancestry were in part surprising and validating. My maternal grandmother, the late Mrs. Minnie Mary Cunningham Murchison McEachern, told my mother, Mrs. Barbara Anne Elizabeth Clyde McEachern Smith, some old family stories about the meeting of my maternal grandmother's parents in South Carolina and their presumed ethnic roots. My great grandmother, Mrs. Hattie Cunningham, was believed to be a full-blooded Native American woman from the Cherokee Nation. She was born and raised in South Carolina. Many members of my father's side of the family, the Smiths, believed that there was some European ancestry in my paternal lineage, and would be revealed in the results of the Patriclan DNA test from African Ancestry. Many of those family members believed that the European ethnicity discovered by the test would be French, believing that they were themselves Creole. I was tested for Matriclan and

Patriclan analysis by African Ancestry in July of 2006 and received the results eight weeks later. The results of my Matriclan test analysis came first. I found out that the stories that my Grandma Minnie told my family about her mother were inaccurate. The results of my African Ancestry Matriclan DNA lineage test revealed that my maternal line, the segment of my Mitochondrial DNA (or X-chromosome) passed down from Grandma Minnie to my mother to me, were surprisingly not Native American in origin, but were indeed African in origin, from the Fulani tribe living in the West African nation of Mali currently, matched to one-hundred percent accuracy. The results of my Patriclan test arrived two weeks later in the mail. My African Ancestry Patriclan test analysis results determined that my paternal line DNA (or Y-chromosome), passed from my paternal grandfather to my father to me, was of European ancestry, however, not of French but of a mixture of German and Irish ethnic origin. My Great-grandfather, Mr. James Morton Smith, was born in Virginia and later moved to West Virginia. He was a coal miner in Appalachia. Many Appalachians were coal miners then. Many of the European-Americans who were coal miners were called Hillbillies of predominantly German heritage. I was surprised to find the Fulani tribal lineage on my maternal line, but the results validated my identity as a Black American of African descent. My paternal line was revealed as of mixed German and Irish lineage, validating the existence and brutal reality of slavery in America, with European male slave owners and their sons producing children with African slave women out of acts of rape, only to have those children be made Black slaves on the White slave masters' plantations. African Ancestry reports that of all Patriclan test results of Black American men, at least thirty percent of those results reveal European ancestry, a chilling reminder of the horrors of slavery in America.

A description of the Fulani Tribe created by African Ancestry (2005) says, "More than half of the Fulani raise livestock. As the Fulani migrated throughout West Africa over the centuries, significant differences emerged among the different groups who considered themselves as Fulani. Most Fulani, known as the Fulani bororo, or 'cattle Fulani,' maintained a traditional pastoral existence. Others, however, known as the Fulani gida, or "town Fulani," took up a settled existence in the towns of kingdoms such as Mali, Songhai, and especially the Hausa states. As Fulani groups migrated, they increasingly adopted forms of Islam practiced by neighboring peoples. These Islamic sects inspired reform movements led by Fulani, often with support from neighboring peoples. They advocated jihad, or holy war, to replace rules perceived as corrupt and greedy with an austere and devout Muslim theocracy. The most famous and powerful of the Fulani theocracies was the Sokoto Caliphate of present-day northern Nigeria. This vast empire arose as the result of a jihad led by a Fulani cleric, Usuman dan Fodio, against the Hausa states during the early 19th century. In each of these states, Fulani gida occupied positions of religious and secular leadership. Fulani remain prominent throughout much of this region today. In northern Nigeria the Fulani gida have gradually merged with wealthy Hausa to form an ethnic group sometimes called Hausa-Fulani. This group remains the effective ruling class of northern Nigeria. Early explorers and researchers noted the cultural and physical differences between the Fulani and neighboring African groups. The Fulani themselves are keenly aware of their distinctive physical appearance: some have relatively fair skin, long hair and aquiline features. The Fulani reckon descent patrilineally; lineage groups form the basis for the social organization of the pastoral Fulani. Especially in herding families, gender roles are well-defined. Younger boys help their older brothers with the herds, while the girls help their mothers. When a boy reaches the age of 12, he enters sukaabe, or 'young adulthood.' At that time, he is taught the rules of respect, courtesy, and justice." The results of my Matriclan and Patriclan DNA lineage tests from African Ancestry were so exciting to find out, and I wanted to know more about my family genetic ethnic lineages. The next person in my family to be tested was my maternal grandfather, Mr. Daniel Robert McEachern.

I purchased a Matriclan test kit and a Patriclan test kit from African Ancestry in the summer of 2007 for my maternal grandfather, Mr. Daniel Robert McEachern, to take to find out his maternal and paternal DNA lineage. My mother swabbed her father's cheeks and we sent in the test kits to see just what we would find. It turned out that the results of these two tests of my grandfather's DNA lineage would be the most interesting of all the DNA test results we have ever received. Discovering the lineage of my maternal grandfather's maternal and paternal lines was important for my family being that my grandfather's father died in World War I after suffering from tuberculosis. My grandfather was a baby and never got to meet or see his biological father. My grandfather's mother was an only child with no siblings and not very much is known about her side of the family either. After the death of my grandfather's father, she remarried and had several other children. Not knowing what to expect from the DNA lineage test results from African Ancestry, we waited for approximately two months until the results finally came. What we found amazed us beyond measure.

The results of my maternal grandfather's DNA maternal lineage test from African Ancestry revealed Native American ancestry through the Asian branch Haplogroup D presently found in South America. The accuracy of the test found a one hundred percent match with my grandfather's DNA.

My maternal grandfather's paternal lineage discovered a one hundred percent match of his DNA with the Yoruba tribe of Nigeria today. My grandfather's humorous response to his maternal and paternal DNA lineage test results from African Ancestry was, "I'm black!!!"

To quote my maternal grandfather's DNA test results explanation (African Ancestry, 2007), "About 60,000 years ago a group of individuals moved out of Africa and their descendents, through the natural process of mutation of mtDNA (mitochondrial DNA), formed the M and N haplogroups. Through time their descendents in Asia, Australia and parts of Europe evolved their own specific types. So, today, Europe is populated by the haplogroups H,I,J,K,T,U,V,W and X; Asia by A,B,C,D,E,F,G,M, and Y; the Americas by the Asian branches A,B,C,D and X; Papua New

Guinea by P and Q; and Australia by further M and N types. The result is that you have inherited through your mother a segment of DNA that was passed on consistently from mother to daughter to you. It is presently found in South America. The Y chromosome DNA sequence that we determined from your sample shares ancestry with the Yoruba people living in Nigeria today."

A description of the Yoruba tribe from the African Nation of Nigeria states (African Ancestry, 2005), "Most Yoruba speakers live in southwestern Nigeria. They form a majority in Lagos, Africa's second most populous city. Yoruba speakers are traditionally among the most urbanized African people. For centuries before British colonization, most Yoruba speakers inhabited a complex, urban society organized around powerful city-states. These densely populated cities centered around the residence of the king, or *oba*. Though they lived in cities, traditionally most Yoruba men farmed crops such as yams, maize, plantains, peanuts, millet, and beans in the surrounding countryside. Many men also engaged in crafts such as blacksmithing, textile manufacturing, and woodworking. Traditionally, Yoruba women specialized in marketing and trade. They could gain considerable independence, status, and wealth through their commercial activity. Yoruba speakers identify themselves as members of several different groups, including the Ife, Isa, and Ketu. All of these groups, however, share a similar material culture, mythology, and artistic tradition. Art historians consider 13th- and 14th century Yoruba bronzes and terra-cotta sculptures among Africa's greatest artistic achievements. Yoruba oral histories, folklore, and proverbs have also won international acclaim. Traditional Yoruba religious beliefs recognize a supreme god presiding over a complex pantheon of hundreds of lesser gods. Over the past several centuries Islam and Christianity have spread to Yorubaland. Many Yoruba take a pluralistic approach to religion that integrates traditional religious elements with Christian and Muslim beliefs, as in the Aladura spiritualist movement. According to folklore, the Yoruba originated from the mythical Olorun, God of the Sky, whose son, Oduduwa, founded the ancient holy city of Ile-Ife around the 8th century C.E. By the 11th century, Ile-Ife was the center of a powerful kingdom. It was one of the earliest to emerge in Africa south of the Sahel. While the institution of kingship probably predates the emergence of Ile-Ife, the holy city became the

preeminent Yoruba spiritual and cultural center.
Another Yoruba city, Oyo, probably originated in the
11th century and became a powerful military state by
the 17th century. The rulers of Oyo acquired horses
by selling enslaved Africans to Europeans and
reselling the manufactured goods to Hausa traders.
Wars among Yoruba groups and city-states raged for
much of the 19th century, leaving many Yoruba
vulnerable to enslavement. Large numbers were sold
to traders who brought them to Latin America. To
this day, Yoruba culture remains influential in Brazil
and Cuba, where Candomble and Santeria religious
practices carry on Yoruba traditions." The next
relative to be tested for maternal and paternal DNA
ethnic genetic lineage was to be my father's mother's
brother, my Uncle Howard Prunty.

In the summer of 2008, my paternal grandmother's brother, my great-uncle Mr. Howard Prunty, agreed to take the African Ancestry Matriclan and Patriclan DNA genetic lineage ancestry tests. Their parents met in Washington, D.C. while studying at Howard University. They almost immediately dated, fell in love, and married. My Great-Grandmother became pregnant with my Grandmother, my Great-Grandparents' first child. They both dropped out of college and moved to West Virginia to start their family. I called African Ancestry to order the tests via phone with my credit card, had the kit sent to the Metro-Atlanta, Georgia area where he lives, and he reimbursed me with a check he sent me in the mail. Uncle Howard agreed to send me copies of the results of the tests in the mail. He sent the test results in the mail and I received them in the fall of 2008. Uncle Howard's Matriclan test results revealed that his maternal line traced back to the Tikar tribe of Cameroon today. His Patriclan test results revealed that his paternal line traced back to a mixture of the Igbo tribe of Nigeria and the Ewondo tribe of Cameroon today. Both tests were found to be one hundred percent accurate. Uncle Howard's Patriclan test results are demonstrative of the mixing of people from different African tribes. Once an African was turned into a slave in America, he was considered separated and ignorant of his African roots, heritage and ancestry. Being slaves, the Black American man would look for a mate who was a Black American of African descent herself, never knowing which African tribe or tribes she and her mate descended from, producing children born into slavery and born without the knowledge of the African tribes and cultures which they came from and belong to. This conscious separation of the Black slave from his and her African past has carried on for over 400 years during slavery in America and also an additional 100 years after slavery including the Jim Crow Era in America, an era of legal segregation and discrimination. This separation from the African Ancestral heritage of the Black American can be reconnected through DNA lineage and admixture tests from companies such as African Ancestry and AncestrybyDNA.

A description of the Tikar tribe from Cameroon reads (African Ancestry, 2005), "Although little is known about the Tikar, they are closely related to other peoples of the Cameroon grasslands, including the Bamileke and the Bamum. They believed to have originally come from the north and migrated to their current location over several centuries. The migration that brought today's grassland inhabitants to Cameroon was often spurred by Fulani traders moving southward into Cameroon in the 17th century. The region was at the center of trade routes that connected Fulani and Hausa traders in the north with the southern port cities. The Tikar were prominent in the region's arts, politics and military for several centuries, making them highly visible and often prime targets for enslavers. The Tikar of Cameroon are closely related to other grassland groups, and share a similar political and familial structure. Villages are governed by single leaders, known as Fon, usually chosen from among the area's ruling families. Every village's Fon is attended by a council of elders who assist him in decision-making. Most Fon serve for an entire lifetime. Traditionally the Tikar are subsistence farmers, growing peanuts, maize and yams and raising chickens and goats. Men clear the fields and hunt, while women – who are thought to make the soil more fruitful – plant and harvest crops. Tikar culture places great emphasis on ancestor worship, and families practice this respect by placing great importance on their forebears' skulls, which may be moved and reburied if the family moves to a new location, or the representation of skulls in masks and other arts. Tikar masks are highly detailed and among the most beautiful in Africa – they are known for strongly defined noses, large almond-shaped eyes, and pointed teeth." Again, the Tikar tribe in Cameroon today was shown as the results of my Uncle Howard's Matriclan test for African Ancestry lineage on his maternal line. The Tikar tribe of Cameroon is a Sub-Saharan West African tribe.

A description of the Igbo tribe in Nigeria shows (African Ancestry, 2005), "The traditional Igbo homeland lies on both sides of the lower Niger River, though most Igbo live to the east of the Niger between the Niger Delta and the Benue Valley. Igboland is one of Africa's most densely populated regions. Although Igbo speakers fall into over a dozen subgroups, they share a common culture and have lived in the same area. Several of Nigeria's leading writers are Igbo, including Chinua Achebe, Cyprian Ekwenis, and Nkem Nwankwo. Until the colonial era most Igbo lived in autonomous, fairly democratic villages, where a complex structure of kinship ties, secret societies, professional organizations, oracles, and religious leaders regulated village society. This mix of overlapping institutions gave most Igbo some decision-making power and prevented any single person from gaining too much power. Europeans arrived in the late 15th century, and by the late 17th century, the area became a major center for the Transatlantic Slave Trade. Many Igbo, especially those living along the Niger River, became traders who sold captives from the interior, including both interior Igbo and members of other ethnic groups. The British (and their North American colonists) played a key role in this trade during the 1700s. From the colonial period onward, the Igbo produced disproportionate numbers of civil servants and military officers. Educated Igbo thus played a central role in the struggle for Nigerian independence. Nigeria's first president, Nnamdi Azikiwe, was an Igbo. The Igbo have a long history of cultural achievement. Traditionally, the Igbo have excelled at metalwork, weaving, and woodcarving. Excavations at the village of Igbo-Ukwu have unearthed sophisticated cast bronze artifacts and textiles dating from the 9th century. Since ancient times, the Igbo have traded craft goods and agricultural products. Traditional Igbo religion varied regionally, but generally included a belief in an afterlife and reincarnation, sacrifice, and spirit and ancestor worship. The Igbo performed elaborate ceremonies marking funerals and other life passages. The decentralization and cultural openness of the Igbo made them prime targets for missionaries. Today most Igbo are Christian, and they have a high literacy rate."

Again, the Igbo tribe from Nigeria is a Sub-Saharan West African tribe. This tribe was one of two African tribes discovered by African Ancestry on the paternal line of my paternal grandmother's brother, my Great-Uncle Howard.

A brief description of the Ewondo tribe in Cameroon articulates (African Ancestry, 2005), "The Ewondo are one of three main subgroups of Beti, themselves a subgroup of the Fang people. They speak a Bantu language and the majority practice Christian faiths. Most live in and around the capital of city of Yaounde (Cameroon), but some Ewondo live in more rural regions in the central and southern provinces of the country. There, the Ewondo are chiefly farmers. Their agricultural system is based on crop rotation, using crops such as groundnuts, cassava, macabo, and cucumber." Again, the Ewondo tribe of Cameroon is a Sub-Saharan West African tribe. This tribe was the second of two

African tribes found to be on the paternal line of my Uncle Howard. The other African tribe discovered was the Igbo tribe. The next relative to be tested was to be my paternal grandfather's sister, my Great-Aunt Shirley.

In the spring of 2009, I ordered a Matriclan test kit from African Ancestry to test my paternal grandfather's sister, my Great-Aunt Shirley. My Great-grandmother, Mrs. Anne Smith was a Black woman who was suspected by the Smith Family to be of Creole heritage. Her mother, according to the Smith Family Legend, was suspected of being a White woman of mixed Irish, French and/or Spanish heritage. Her father was suspected to be a Black slave. Aunt Shirley and her children and grandchildren believed that Aunt Shirley's mother's mother was a woman of European heritage. Because her last name was O'Neal, her ethnicity was presumed to be Irish. Still other members of the family believed that she actually was a woman of African descent who just had a very fair skin complexion. An old picture of this family ancestor showed that she could be identified as a white woman. If she indeed was a woman of African descent, her very fair complexion could have allowed her to pass for a white woman. A Matriclan test from African Ancestry would determine if my paternal grandfather's mother's mother, my Great-Great Grandmother Ms. O'Neal, was an Irishwoman or a woman of African descent. If the test results proved her to be a woman of African descent, African Ancestry would be able to find which tribe and from which African nation the tribe was from that would match my Aunt Shirley's mtDNA. In the summer of 2009, the DNA test results came via mail. The results package would reveal that my Aunt Shirley had on her maternal line a 98.9% match with the Yoruba tribe in Nigeria. The results proved that the ancestor in question, Aunt Shirley's mother's mother, originally believed by Aunt Shirley to be an Irishwoman, was indeed a woman of African descent, related to the Yoruba tribe in Nigeria today to a statistically significant 98.9% accuracy. The test results are symbolic of the perceived and actual interracial sexual relations between Black people and White people. The perception was that Black men and White women were involved sexually as much as White men and Black women were involved sexually during slavery in America. The reality is that very rarely if at all did Black men as slaves get sexually involved with White women. Most of the time the sexual involvement of Black people with White people during slavery in America occurred with forced sexual encounters with Black slave women by White male slave owners and White male family members of slave owners. The statistic of African

Ancestry shows a thirty-percent occurrence among Black American men of European ancestry on the paternal line and African ancestry on the maternal line, with little if any occurrence of African ancestry on the paternal line and European ancestry on the maternal line of Black American men dating back to the time of slavery in America. Aunt Shirley's Matriclan DNA test results proved a valuable lesson learned to that effect from African Ancestry. The next person to be tested would be my maternal grandmother's brother's son, my cousin Rev. James Oscar Cunningham.

In November of 2010 I ordered a Patriclan test kit from African Ancestry to test my maternal grandmother's brother's son, my cousin Rev. James Oscar Cunningham. I took the test kit down to North Carolina with my mother and father for two weeks, spending the entire Thanksgiving Day Holiday Weekend with my mother's brother, Uncle Butch. Before going on the trip I talked with my mother's sister, Aunt Marilyn, to arrange a date, time and place to test my cousin Oscar. We met up with him at my Aunt Marilyn's place and tested him there. We sent in the test kit via mail to African Ancestry and two months later we got the results.

The family story of my mother's mother's father, my Great-Grandfather Bob Cunningham, was that he immigrated by rowing a banana boat from Jamaica to South Carolina, U.S.A., where he met

Mrs. Hattie Cunningham, my Great-Grandmother, who was presumably a full-blooded Cherokee Native American woman. Another family story was that my mother's mother's father, my Great-Grandfather Mr. Bob Cunningham, was a man of European descent, identified as a son of a White slave master. We found out that my Great-Grandmother, my mother's mother's mother, was not of the Cherokee tribe of Native American descent, but actually she was a Black American woman of African descent. This we know now having tested myself on my maternal line with a Matriclan test from African Ancestry. We found that my mtDNA was matched with one hundred percent accuracy to the Fulani tribe in Mali today, a Sub-Saharan African tribe in West Africa today.

The test results of my cousin Oscar's Patriclan test from African Ancestry were that on his paternal line, his DNA on his Y chromosome was a one hundred percent match with the Akan tribe in Ghana today, a Sub-Saharan African tribe in West Africa today. These test results proved that my Great-Grandfather, Mr. Bob Cunningham, was not a White male slave master of European descent but he indeed was a Black man of African descent. The story of my mother's mother's father arriving in South Carolina, U.S.A. from Jamaica on a banana boat could actually be true, given that the Nation of Jamaica did have Black slaves of African descent during the period of slavery in America. My Great-Grandfather could have left Jamaica looking for a life of freedom from British rule that transpired for a number of years in Jamaica, even after slavery was abolished in Jamaica.

It was invigorating for me to find just what the paternal lineage was for my Great-Grandfather, Mr. Bob Cunningham, through testing the DNA on the Y chromosome of my Cousin Oscar, which turned out to be one hundred percent related to the Akan tribe in Ghana today.

A description of the Akan tribe in Ghana today reveals (African Ancestry, 2005), "The broad Akan grouping includes a number of separate ethnic groups, who share several cultural traits but have their own histories and customs. The main Akan ethnicities include the Akyem, Akwamu, Asante, Brong, Denkyira, Fante, Nzima, Sefwi, and Wassa of Ghana, and the Baule and Anyi of Ivory Coast. Linguistic and archaeological evidence suggests that ancestors of the Akan have inhabited a heartland in south central Ghana for at least 2000 years. The early

Akan lived in agricultural villages raising yams, plantains and millet and sorghum in the north. Many Akan also hunted, worked metals such as iron and gold, and wove baskets and cloth. During the 14th century, the Brong were the first Akan people to form a powerful kingdom, known as Bono. Bono introduced standard gold weights made of brass, later adopted by other Akan nations, for use in the gold trade. With the arrival of Portuguese on the coast during the late 15th century, Akan groups began to expand south toward the coast to trade directly with the Europeans. It was the Asante who built the strongest Akan state, which dominated most of what is now Ghana from about 1700 until the British finally conquered it in 1900. Today Akan peoples number more than 10 million, almost half of Ghana's population. They are primarily agriculturalists, farming cash crops such as cocoa and coffee along with subsistence crops such as yams and plantains. They have occupied prominent political offices in both Ghana and the Ivory Coast. Ghana's first president, Kwame Nkrumah, was an Akan of Nzima origin, and Ivory Coast's independence leader, Felix Houphouet-Boigny, was a Baule. In ancient times, headmen governed rural villages. Some scholars say that even small units had queen mothers and kings who ruled with the assistance of a council of elders. Traditionally, Akan societies trace descent – including inheritance, kinship ties, and succession – matrilineally, or through the mother's line, though spiritual attributes and certain offices may pass patrilineally, or through the father's line. All Akan societies comprise a seven or eight matrilineal clans, or *abusua*. Patrilineal groupings, the *ntoro*, also control certain taboos and rituals. Traditionally, Akan peoples worship a supreme being, Nyame. His children or creations form a secondary group of lesser deities, *abosom*, which inhabit everyday objects. Priests derive their power from the third level of supernatural entities the talismans. Although many Akan today retain traditional beliefs, Christianity is a major force in Akan society, especially in the south. Muslim influence is stronger in the north." Again, the Akan tribe in Ghana today is a Sub-Saharan African tribe in West Africa today. The Patriclan test of mother's mother's brother's son, my cousin Rev. James Oscar Cunningham from African Ancestry was the final DNA lineage test in my eight lineage DNA tests from African Ancestry. The maximum number of DNA lineage bloodlines that one person can discover for oneself for one's family by using African

Ancestry is eight. By testing myself and four other relatives I found a total of eight lineage bloodlines running through my veins. Six of the eight lineage tests revealed African ancestry, while one lineage test showed Native American ancestry of Asian origin and another lineage test discovering European ancestry. I was now finished with the DNA lineage tests thanks in huge part to my family and African Ancestry. It was now time to find out an estimate of my overall ethnic ancestry by examining my entire DNA code through an admixture test administered by the organization AncestrybyDNA.

The next genetic ethnic DNA test that I was to take was the DNA admixture test administered by AncestrybyDNA, a company parented by the DNA Diagnostics Center (DDC) in southwestern Ohio. This test was a more generalized estimate of my overall biogeographical ancestry analyzed into four different biogeographical ethnic groups: European, Indigenous American, Sub-Saharan African and East Asian. The test examines your entire DNA and estimates by percentage which biogeographical ancestral groups match your DNA with 98% confidence intervals. I ordered my admixture test from AncestrybyDNA, had my cheeks swabbed and mailed in my test kit to AncestrybyDNA in February of 2011 and received my results via mail from AncestrybyDNA at the end of March 2011. The results were printed on a certificate that revealed the results of the test. The test results discovered in my DNA were an estimate of a biogeographical ancestral admixture of 78% Sub-Saharan African, 18% European, 4% East Asian and 0% Indigenous American. The DNA admixture test results gathered by AncestrybyDNA were fairly close to the findings of the lineage tests discovered by African Ancestry, with six of eight (75% of) ancestral bloodlines having African Ancestry. Also, the AncestrybyDNA/African Ancestry results comparison found European ancestry estimated (18% estimated) by AncestrybyDNA and one of eight (or 12.5% of) ancestral bloodlines showing European ancestry found by African Ancestry's DNA lineage tests. East Asian estimates of 4% and Indigenous American estimates of 0% were found by AncestrybyDNA compared to one of eight (or 12.5% of) ancestral bloodlines revealed

Native American ancestry of Asian origin. My father, Mr. Morton V. Smith, Jr., also agreed to take the AncestrybyDNA admixture test. I ordered the test for him in April of 2011. My father swabbed himself and mailed in his test kit at the end of May 2011. He received his test results in the second week of July 2011. My father's DNA admixture test results revealed an estimated biogeographical ancestral admixture of 75% Sub-Saharan African, 22% European, 3% East Asian and 0% Indigenous American. His admixture test results were close to mine showing a little less Sub-Saharan African, a little more European and very close to the same amount of East Asian (3% percent for my father compared to 4% for myself), and both admixture test result estimates revealing 0% Indigenous American.

A brief description of how the AncestrybyDNA admixture test results are interpreted demonstrates (AncestrybyDNA, DDC, 10-13), "The AncestrybyDNA test reports estimates of your biogeographical ancestry... Your results come in two formats: a table report listing your ancestral percentages of the four founder groups (European, Sub-Saharan African, East Asian, and Indigenous American)... An important concept to understand when interpreting your results is the maximum likelihood estimate or MLE... With a genetic test, ancestry can only be estimated in a statistical sense, much like the track of a hurricane... Therefore, it is not possible to determine what your proportions are exactly... In conclusion, the result of our test is your MLE... The test results provide ancestral estimates for the four founding populations: European,

Indigenous American, Sub-Saharan African, and East Asian... European... This people group includes Europeans, Middle Easterners, and South Asians... Indigenous American... This group is composed of people who migrated to inhabit North, South and Central America... Sub-Saharan African... This group includes people with roots in the Sub-Saharan region of Africa... East Asian... This people group includes the Japanese, Chinese, Koreans, and Pacific Islanders... As you can tell from the brief descriptions, the names of the four founding populations listed in your test results in are used in a simplistic sense. It is important to remember that these 'founding populations' really refer to a group of people with shared ancestry who occupy certain geopolitical areas with 'blurred boundaries.'"

These two DNA admixture tests administered by AncestrybyDNA conclude my research of my family ancestry via DNA testing. In all ten tests were administered to myself and six other relatives, revealing eight of my family DNA lineage bloodlines and the DNA genetic biogeographical ancestral admixture of myself and my father.

Now I know the race and ethnicity of eight of my ancestral bloodlines and the admixture of my biogeographical composition along with my father's admixture of biogeographical composition. I intend to tell all of my family about the results of these DNA tests and about how the results validate my identity as a Black man of African descent. And as a Black man of African descent, I can claim the actual tribes of people and nations of Africa from whom I descend. The Fulani people in Mali today, the Yoruba and Ibo peoples in Nigeria today, the Tikar and Ewondo peoples in Cameroon today, and the Akan people in Ghana today are all Black African peoples with whom I share DNA. These peoples also share with me relation to the same ancestors of the ancient Motherland of Africa to the exact tribes and nations. Without African Ancestry, I still would not know which African tribes, nations and bloodline roots my forefathers descended from to accent my ancestral family tree. I also know that the admixture of my biogeographical DNA along with my father's to illustrate a summary of percentages of Sub-Saharan African, European, East Asian and Indigenous American bloodlines. My admixture, along with my father's, showed predominantly Sub-Saharan African genealogy with significant amounts of European genealogy and small portions of East Asian genealogy with absolutely no percentages of Indigenous American genealogy. I know that there is no Native American blood in my family. I also know that my paternal bloodline shows European ancestry, consistent with 30% of the Black African-American male population, a strong reminder of the harsh realities and horrors of the peculiar institution of slavery in America. I also discovered a percentage of East Asian DNA admixture, an ancestral link previously unknown to my family. I feel better knowing why I am a Black-American man of African descent. Now endowed with proof of this identity through DNA evidence, I can share my familial ancestral stories and teach others how to do so also. I can, without my doubt in my mind, body or soul, profess the truth of my familial ancestry. I can now join in with the catch phrase made an anthem of my people by the late great Godfather of Soul James Brown, beyond a shadow of a doubt, "Say it loud, I'm Black and I'm proud!!!" I thank all of my family, friends and God the most for allowing me to discover the truth about my familial ancestry, a treasure that can be shared with others for generations to come and to inspire all who seek to know the truth about their own genealogical familial ancestral bloodlines and roots to capture a portrait of their own family trees.

I fulfilled my search for my own family roots and bloodlines and lineage through DNA research. The process and research has proved helpful in identifying my family roots and bloodlines and lineage as a Black American of African descent. I have gained priceless knowledge of myself and of my family heritage and history. Everything as to my looks, my personality, my preferences, my culture, my history and my identity as a Black American of African descent has been affirmed and validated through this research process. Ancestral family bond once broken by the bondage of slavery in America are rediscovered and restored to me and my family. I am glad to have found out everything I did find out about my ancestral roots and family heritage. I can say that being proud of being a Black American of African descent that I found my ancestral family connection and lineage, and hopefully I can inspire other Black people of African descent to do so through my research. You will not only know more, but you will feel better about yourself and your family, your roots, ancestry and your future and destiny as a Black person of African descent. Thanks to my family, both related and extended, and to African Ancestry and AncestrybyDNA, I can say that after discovered my family history and ancestry, I can definitely and surely think, feel, say and express the famous and true James Brown slogan, "Say it loud, I'm Black and I'm proud!!!"